Speaking from the Soul: Poems From Places Yet Explored

Bre O'Brien

Presentation by *BookLeaf Publishing*

Web: www.bookleafpub.com

E-mail: info@bookleafpub.com

ISBN: 9789357214704

First edition 2023

*To those who feel like you're never truly
seen. I see you.*

ACKNOWLEDGEMENT

A huge thank you to Cameron who has pushed me more than I've ever been pushed. I love you more than you'll ever know.

Thank you to everyone else who has helped me grow and change from what I thought I wanted to be.

PREFACE

As a writer, I have spent many hours, days, years creating characters and speaking through them. I have voiced them, brought them to life, but my own voice has been muffled in the background. Recently, I've begun to miss the experiences I have shunned in place of writing. I've had to acknowledge shortcomings and face growth in ways that have been uncomfortable because I have never been fully in tune with me. I'm a people pleaser, and because of that, I carry many regrets.

Please enjoy the journey through my innermost self.

Who Am I?

When I was born, I had so much potential,
A blank canvas yet to experience the world.
My parents had such high hopes for me.
So where did it all go wrong?

I never liked my full name as a kid.
It wasn't as cute or as soft as some of the other
girls' names.
It wasn't timeless, or cute.
It never rolled off the tongue like some.
Three full syllables with jutting starts and
repeated letters.
I could never write my N's the right way.

It was easier to pretend to be someone else,
A beautiful redhead from a cartoon,

The name of a flower, timeless and never out of
style.
My birth month, a name for an older lady, but
also just as timeless.
Those names, no one could make fun of.
With those names, I could escape.

As I grew, one person was able to say my name,
Such beauty, such grace, such poetry fell from
his lips.
I craved my name then,
And when I received it, as rare as it was,
I finally began to feel alive.

After that,
After he and I went our separate ways,
I wanted to be anything but my name.
I was the breeze.
Then I was a type of cheese,
After that I lost my spark and had no name,
Just a face hiding the truth.
I was a single letter.

Finally, after years,
I chose my own name.
I chose a nickname that I love.

Hi, my name is Bre.
Let me entertain you.

Who Do I Want to Be?

When I was little, I wanted to be a cat.
I had a Halloween costume from when I was
three,
And I thought that was all I needed.

"Daddy, I'm a cat".

In Elementary School, I wanted to be a princess.
I would watch Princess movies for hours,
Pretend my too-large sleep shirt was a ball
gown.

"Mommy, I'm a princess."

When I was seven, maybe eight, I was
introduced to writing.
The first attempts were with gel-pen on black
paper.
The ink shone like diamonds on the page with
my illegible handwriting.
But the idea followed me around before I even
knew what I wanted.

When I was a little older,
Watching the "Cosby Show" with my dad,
I wanted to be a doctor or a lawyer.
"Why not both?" I said to myself,
Reaching for the highest goals I could.

Before my self-confidence and self-worth was
torn away.

When I was ten, at a new school with new
friends,
I wanted to be a Super-Star.
Singer, Dancer, Artist.
The art bug had bitten me and I began to write
when no one was looking.

I wrote of all the beautiful things I experienced
when I lived away from home,
I wrote of the injustices I thought I was
enduring.
All of the family was nice, except the "sister"
who had been forced upon me.

"Everything is the opposite"
I'm still not sure they believed me.

At Fourteen, my true dream was realized.
The spark of an idea bit me in history class.
Writing was all I could think about.
Fleshing out the idea onto paper, was like a drug.
But I didn't tell anyone.
It was my secret alone.

At Seventeen, I wrote again.
But this time, it was different.
Junior year was hard.
The subject I loved was torture,
So I turned inward instead.

I wrote,
And wrote,
And wrote.

But had nothing to show for it.
No one thought it would be a good career.

At Eighteen, I wanted to go to college for
writing.
My dad, my only support,
Did not support me.

"You should be a nurse."

With no extra money, no SAT scores to pad my
application,
I was all but forced to community college to be a
nurse.

At 19, I was a CNA,
But still writing.

At 20, I was on the wait-list,
But still writing.
That year I started writing a new series,
One that I still hope to sell one day.

At 21, I started the LVN program.
I lost my mother that year,
But not before she gave me the best gift.

She printed the fruit of my labors,
Handed it to me in a large paper-box.

"I love it, Honey."

At 23, I graduated from the RN program.
Still writing, still creating,
In hopes of making something great.

"I am a Registered Nurse"
But it never felt quite right to say out loud.
It never sounded genuine.

Ages 24-29, I worked all manner of nursing
jobs.
They weren't all bad,
But it is taxing being something you're not.
It's soul-sucking to work at something you don't
enjoy.

At 30, my life changed.
I grew up.
I moved out.
Started a new life, new job, new school,
And started doing what I wanted.

I am going to be a published writer, no matter
what it takes.
I am a writer,
I am going to do what I love.

"I am an Author."

Mom

Mom labored for 27 hours to birth me,
But didn't get to see my 22nd birthday.

She begged for a child,
because her friends were all having kids,
But when it came time to raise me,
She gave her love and attention to drugs instead.

For most of my life,
She was more of a stranger,
Than what a mother should be.

I had several motherly influences growing up.
They did the best they could,
But they could never replace who should have
been there.

The last few years of her life,
I reached out,
But it was never enough.

We were just starting to get somewhere,
And then it was all over.

I've spent a lot of time with my thoughts since
then.
Thinking about what was,
What could have been,
And more importantly,
What could never be.

As I get older now,
I wonder how I will fare as a mother.
With no true influence,
No day-to-day woman in my life.
The one thing I craved for so long.

Hug your mothers,
Because there are so many of us who no longer
can.

Dad

What can I say about my dad?

How about the fact that he did whatever he
could to raise me?
How about how much he gave up for me and my
sister (who never did appreciate it the way I
did)?

My dad, who gave up everything to raise his
daughters.
My dad, who spent months fighting in court,
years fighting for finances, and decades getting
nothing in return.

My dad is my hero, in the best ways and the
worst ways.
He is what I have always looked for in a man,
But never quite found.

He is what I know not to look for in a man,
Because I know I would break his heart.

My dad, who has been nothing but kind,
Doesn't deserve the lot he's been handed.
Doesn't deserve the pain he's had to go through.

My dad put me through school, even when
finances were tough.
He made use of the money spread so thin,
That even I don't know how it was possible.

He made it happen, at the expense of his own
dreams.
He made it happen, at the expense of his own
life.
He made it happen, despite the odds.

For that, I am thankful.

My dad, who I've been told is the male version
of me,
more like it's vice versa.
I am my father's daughter.
Through the thick and thin of it,
I can't change my make-up.

But I can try to rise above it all and succeed.

The One Who Got Away

I have vague memories of you,
The one who got away.
Shadows in my memories,
Blonde hair in the corner,
Half-braided as blood spills from your nose.

There are few pictures of you around,
But maybe that's a good thing.
I'm not sure I could handle it,
If our roles were reversed.

I remember the fights,
The complaints,
The teenage angst emanating from you,
When I was a toddler and desperate to be as cool
as you.

For the few years of my childhood you were
there,
You were mostly a stranger.
Dad tells stories of the strife with your mother,
The strife she planted in you,
And the strife that still remains.

For years, you were like a secret.
A small tidbit that I never told.
An invisible friend would have been more
believable,
But you do belong to me,
However distant we are.

However uncaring you are about us,
Until you need something.
I'm here,
But don't expect me to open the door so easily.

Sister.

The Comparison Game

As a child,
I looked forward to the Holidays.
The warmth of homemade food for
Thanksgiving,
The warm glow of the lights shining on the
wrapping paper under the tree at Christmas.
I would dress up in the best dresses I had,
Wear the shiniest shoes,
Like it was the best day for dress-up ever.

And then,
Everything changed.

As soon as the kids were all old enough,
The parents would play the comparison game.
"Your child goes to public school,
Mine goes to private."
"My kids have two loving parents,
While you raise your daughter on your own."

The unfortunate part,
The comparison game was passed down to the
children too
"She got here first, so we're going to play
together,
No room for a third."
"You're a weirdo."
"Stop copying me!"

When you're a kid,
Words hurt more than you can ever tell your
parents.
Holidays, the things I once loved,
Became a battleground.
A rush to get there first so I could have a
companion for the duration.

We were always late.

So from that, I became a chameleon.
I made the rounds,
Talked to the adults,
Wore my maturity like a set of armor.
I didn't give in to the comparison game.

I still don't.

Now, holidays are spent with people who care.
A family I have been invited into,
A family that doesn't need to play the
comparison game,
Because we are all on the same level.

I am forever grateful.

Becoming What I Was Born to Be

There isn't much I remember from my
childhood.
I never had the ideal nuclear family,
I never had a stuffed animal that I cherished,
I never had a loving mother to nurture me.

I'm glad there are no pictures of that time.
I don't think I would have been happy in any of
them,

Or if I was, I doubt the smile would be genuine.
The second grade school picture,
Where I'm scowling sums up what I remember
of those years.

Except…

That was the year that I found my destiny. I
simply didn't know it yet.

The benefit of having a few friends older than
you:
Knowledge of what is to come.
At seven, I had no desire to sit around and listen
to music,
Too much nervous energy.
But the minute the paper and gel pens came out,
That was when I found my calling.

The first writings were rudimentary,
Large neophyte letters, uneven on the lines,
With a drawing taking up more than half the
page.

But the more I wrote, the more the ideas swirled
around in my head.
A handful of ideas kept me occupied for months,
Until I moved away from creating when my
world was once again shaken.

The year away from home, at ten years old,
Where I did have the idea nuclear family,
Where I did have toys and games that weren't in
danger of creeping mold,
Where I had a loving mother figure to nurture
me,
Where I met most of the friends I have now.

That year formed me and shaped me into the
person I am today.
That year, I struggled
But I found coping in writing.
I didn't realize how important it was until much
later.

At thirteen,
I realized my dream of being a writer.
An idea from a U.S. History class,
Formed an idea in my head that I still hold close.
One full novel later, but the edits killed the
dream.

At seventeen,
A school assignment turned into a full-length
novel,
Read page by page to an unenthusiastic,
but overly pleasing teen crush.
Now I cringe when I read it.

At eighteen,
Another novel idea,
Written over the last year of high school,
My "Magnum Opus".
Written in erasable pen.

At twenty,
I started writing a novel series in composition
notebooks,
Typed it up,
Edited it too many times,
But the writing spark was truly born.

I haven't stopped since and I don't intend to stop
anytime soon.

At Thirty-One,
I'm sitting here,
Branching out.
Writing Poetry,
Spilling my secrets and blood on the page:
Making myself heard.

To Care

Relaxation is a foreign word,
Something that never really seems to stay.
Calm is an app on my phone,
Breathing is something quick and hurried.

Tension and Worry have made a home in my
body,
Twisting and corrupting the muscles,
Until they sing the constant song of pain,
Until they bend under the weight of the world,
And never care to go back to the way they once
were.

The baggage I unwillingly carry,
The heavy load of grief and guilt,
Shouldn't be mine.
But I can't seem to let it go,
Because I already feel I'm too aloof.

Someone needs to care,
And that someone is me,
Even if it comes with the cost of my own comfort.

Checks and Balances

Money has never been a friend of mine.
From not having enough of it,
To not knowing how to handle it.
We have never been on the same page.

My parents struggled with money,
My grandparents never spoke of money,
But they all pretended like money was never an
issue.

Until it was too late.

My father supported me and loved me,
Despite financial troubles.
So I support him and love him,
Despite his financial struggles.

From the time I could work,
I did what I could
To make sure I would never be in the same
financial struggles.

Yet here I am.

There have been times in my career
Where the checks were significant.
The first check I ever made,
Just short of $900,
The most money I'd ever held in my life.
The last check of my first nursing job,
Just short of $800,
Which meant it was time to go.
Now this most recent check,
Just short of $700,
Means it's time to move on.

Despite how much I love the job I'm in.
That kind of money won't support me
Nor will it support my future.

It's time to grow up and face the truth,
A salary is the price you pay,
For your dreams to lay dormant.

Off to work I go.

To Be Loved

All I've ever wanted is to be loved,
And feel loved.

It started with my parents,
Never truly in love in the first place,
Merely thrust together by the circumstance of
me.

My mother left,
My father did the best he could.
But I always felt like there was something
missing.

The few times I remember seeing my mother,
She flitted from boyfriend to boyfriend,
Like a hummingbird, never staying at a single
flower too long.
I suppose she was looking for love too.

So I did the same.

It started in elementary school,
With the boyfriends who weren't really
boyfriends,
But a name I could claim,
A shelter in the storm that never was anything
real.

In fifth grade,
I met the boy,
Who turned into the man,
I thought I would spend the rest of my life with.
But instead of starting a schoolyard romance,
I ran around with other boys and loved him from
afar.

In middle school,
With the raging hormones,
New body parts and the awkwardness of a baby
deer,
I had a few "boyfriends".
One of them gave me my first kiss,

My first slow dance,
But nothing much else.

High school was tricky.
I had "boyfriends" that never really amounted to
anything.
I set two friends against one another in search of
affection,
And picked neither of them.
Then, when I turned 16,
The boy from fifth grade,
Now a strapping man of 16,
Became my first official boyfriend.

Our relationship was all I had ever dreamed of,
Love, affection, laughter,
Even if we did move at a snail's pace.
But like all good things,
It had to come to an end.

Instead of love for me,
And plans for the future,
His love of religion won out.

The college years,
I would like to label the "Loser Era".
In those handful of years,
I attached myself to anyone

Who could give me what I had lost after high
school.
No one measured up.

Instead of love,
I got trauma,
Anxiety,
Illness,
And more religious bullshit than I could
stomach.

But there was one man in that era,
The man who would never be my type,
But who gave me more love than I probably
deserved,
Until the monster called Anxiety invaded it all,
And stole him away.

I couldn't handle it,
And I never apologized,
But I still think of him sometimes.
I wonder where we would be if I had stayed.

But I try not to let those thoughts get the better
of me,
What's in the past,
Is in the past.
I made my choices for the betterment of me.

The last guy,
So full of delusions of a relationship,
So attached at the hip to his mother's beck and
call.
So withholding of love and affection,
But dangling just enough to make me wait,
Was the last in a long line of "losers".

No, we were not in a relationship.
No, we were never in a relationship.
No, a relationship cannot be so secret that even
your partner doesn't know about it.

Yes, experimentation happened in the back of
cars,
But no words of affection were exchanged,
No signs of any kind of a relationship,
Not until I said I was interested in someone else,
And it was all too late.

The last man,
Ironically,
Someone I also met in fifth grade.
We went all through school,
Had crushes on each other at different times,
But never acted on them.

At the ten-year high school reunion,
He was one of the only people I recognized.

We talked about how our lives had changed,
Talked about where we were going.

From text messages,
Came in-person meetings,
And we formed a relationship.

Now I truly feel like I'm loved,
The way I deserve to be loved.

Doodle and the Breeze

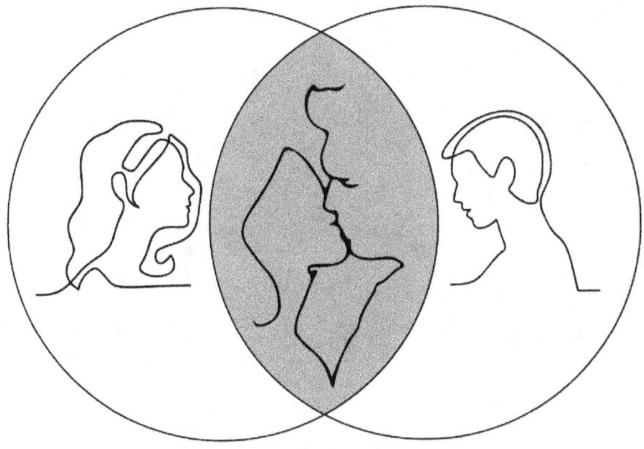

There once was a Button named Doodle
Who spent all his time being truthful.

There once was a Bucket named Breeze,
Who spent all her time trying to please.

As children, Doodle and Breeze had met on the
playground,
But Life had a way of throwing them around.

Until one evening, a party was thrown,
For the Buttons and the Buckets that had already
grown.

Now there at the party, the two they did meet,
She talked of work, he talked of a most brave
feat.

But as with the Buttons and Buckets of yore,
In steps a Crack, thinking highly of himself, but
is really a bore.

The Crack tried to woo Breeze with tales of his
magic,
But Breeze saw right through it, it was really
quite tragic.

Now Doodle sat back and watched the crack
talk,
But Doodle himself knew he was the cock of the
walk.

Later that night, over libations a plenty,
Doodle and Breeze accounted for years past
twenty.

After the night came to an end too quick,
Doodle kept talking to Breeze, he was really
quite slick.

For weeks they did meet and speak,
And for quite a time they had quite a streak.

As weeks turned to months, Breeze did realize,
Her life was better with Doodle by her side.

Doodle set up a plan and they took a vacation,
Both heading off to a nice beach location.

To dinner, the aquarium and shopping they did
go,
And as the days went by, Breeze started to know.

Up on a rooftop, near the warmth of a fire and
under the stars, with wind through their hair,
Doodle asked Breeze if they could be a pair.

At 11:11 on January 11th, his wish did come
true.
Now the two are inseparable, as lovebirds often
do.

Ring

A ring is a thing,
That much happiness would bring.

A ring on a phone,
To see if someone is home.

A ring of a bell,
To wish everyone well.

A ring on a finger,
To make happiness linger.

A ring as a promise of things yet to come,
A ring on the finger for the keys to the kingdom.

A ring as a sign of love and devotion,
A sure sign of things forever in motion.

A ring from my love,
With the stars shooting above,
Surely means more joy is to come.

Touched

Death has touched you
with her long slender fingers
and now you see her everywhere.

You see her face everywhere you turn,
in mothers and children and dirty old men,
and like a hounded lover, you cannot escape her.

She is like the girlfriend you wish you never
had,
She keeps you up at night for nothing fun,
and during the day likes to hide just outside your
field of vision.

She is your own personal terrorist,
and yet,
She is only there to comfort you.

Medicine

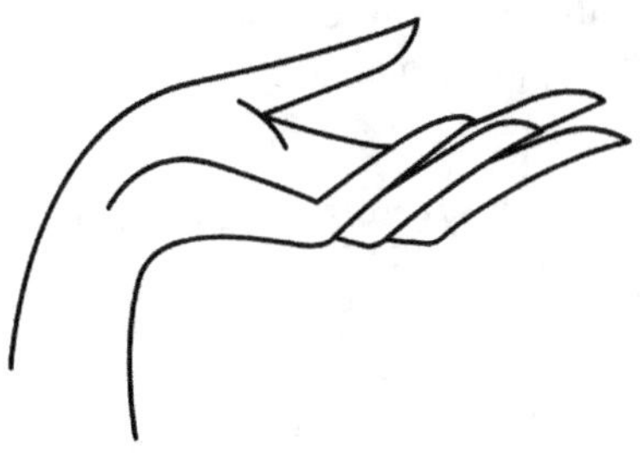

To the first I gave truths,
The means and the way to best navigate the
waters.

The second received acceptance,
Strength to face the daily challenges of war.

The third was given time,
And in the blink of an eye it was gone.

The fourth received all the praise in the world,
But spent it on all the wrong things.

The next received friendship,
Daily words of comfort.

They all no longer matter as much as
You do now.

What can the nurse give you?
What will you take?

All good little boys must take their medicine.

To Fall

Just when I think I'm stable,

When I can stand on my own two feet,

Be strong,

You barrel into me.

Knock me off balance,

Like a house of cards,

The Tower of Babel,

A sandcastle yielding to the waves.

What you don't realize,

I will come back stronger than ever.

One day,

Your force won't bother me.

To Lose

Rapid breaths,
Not herself when the attacks come.
Six rings of the telephone,
And no response.
Blinking lights,
Rapid responses.
This is how you say goodbye to a friend.

What is normal
After so much has changed
In a short time?
Why does grief always come
with a side of hashbrowns,
Or waffles?

To Work

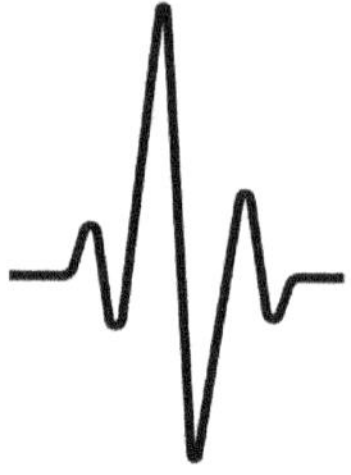

Slow moving doctors,
Speeding nurses,
Sleeping patients,
And I am sick to my stomach
From no breakfast,
A small dinner
And trying to keep up.

When each patient takes more than they need,
And every nurse is depleted a little bit more,
When hours are long and mostly unrewarded.
A hot bath is in order.
Still, the muse is as elusive as ever.

To Grow

I feel I am molten,

Lava bubbling and shifting just beneath my skin,

Waiting to erupt forth in a brilliant spectacle of despair,

And rebirth.

My muscles can't stay stagnant,

My blood courses with new vigor,

My body ready to awaken,

And create something beautiful.